What's the Earth made of?

Susan Mayes

Designed by Lindy Dark
Illustrated by Stuart Trotter and Chris Shields
Science consultant: Ben Spencer
Cover design by Russell Punter
Cover illustration by Christyan Fox
With thanks to Sarah Cronin

CONTENTS

Planet Earth

The Earth is a planet which is made mostly of rock. It spins around the Sun in a part of space called the Solar System. There are nine planets in the Solar System altogether.

The Solar System

This picture shows the planets in the Solar System. Each one moves around the Sun on its own invisible path called an orbit.

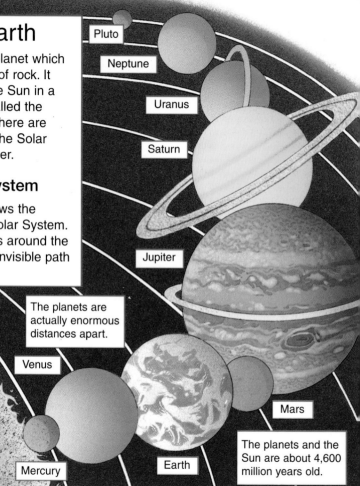

Pluto

Neptune

Uranus

Saturn

Jupiter

The planets are actually enormous distances apart.

Venus

Mars

Sun

Mercury

Earth

The planets and the Sun are about 4,600 million years old.

The beginning

The Earth probably began as a huge, swirling cloud of dust and gases.

Then, the cloud started to shrink. It turned into a spinning ball of hot, runny rock.

The surface cooled and hardened into a rocky crust. Clouds formed and rain fell to make seas.

Inside and outside

The Earth is made up of layers. The thin outer layer is called the crust. It is solid rock. Underneath, there is a very thick, hot layer of rock, called the mantle.

The Earth's middle is called the core. It is hot, runny metal on the outside and solid metal on the inside. The inside is the hottest part of our planet.

Crust

Mantle

Outer core

Inner core

Internet link Go to *www.usborne-quicklinks.com* for a link to a website where you can investigate the Earth's layers as a junior geologist.

3

The big jigsaw

The Earth's crust is not one whole piece, like the skin of an apple. It is made of separate pieces which fit together closely, like a giant jigsaw puzzle. These pieces are called plates.

This flat model shows how the plates fit together.

Sea covers a lot of each plate. Land is the high part of a plate which sticks out of the water.

The edges of the plates are called plate boundaries.

Mantle

Land

Sea

How thick is the crust?

The crust is about 5km (3 miles) thick in some places and 70km (43 miles) thick in others. It is very thin compared with what is underneath. If the Earth was the size of a soccer ball, the crust would only be as thick as a piece of paper.

Floating plates

The plates float on the mantle. In the mantle there is hot, sticky liquid rock, called magma. The magma churns around and makes the plates move.

Internet link Go to *www.usborne-quicklinks.com* for a link to a website where you can watch Pangea splitting up and find out more about the Earth's crust.

Before and after

Some scientists think that 200 million years ago, the plates were joined so that the land was one huge piece. They call it Pangea.

Pangea

The world today

As the plates moved around, Pangea began to split up. The pieces of land drifted apart very slowly and became the shapes we see on maps today.

Fossil clues

Fossils are the remains of animals and plants that died long ago. The same kinds have been found far apart. This is probably because the land they once lived on separated.

Lystrosaurus was a prehistoric animal. Its fossilized remains have been found in countries far apart.

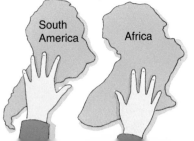

South America

Africa

Fitting together

To see how the Earth's land used to fit together, trace the shapes of South America and Africa from a map of the world and cut them out. Can you tell where the countries used to join?

The changing crust

The Earth's plates move around very slowly. If one plate moves, the ones around it move, too. This makes the crust change in different ways.

Mountains

The world's highest mountain ranges are made when two plates crash into each other. The crust is pushed up into huge folds, called fold mountains.

Make your own

To make a fold mountain, roll out three rectangles of Plasticine* and sandwich them together. Push the ends inward and see how a fold appears.

*US = modeling clay

Layers of folded rock

Folded rock

You can sometimes see rock with folds in it, in cliffs and mountain sides.

Internet links Go to **www.usborne-quicklinks.com** for links to websites where you can see animations that show how mountains are formed.

Up and down

Plates often move apart under the sea. Magma comes up through the crack. It hardens into a ridge of new crust.

Ridges of new crust

Magma rising

Mantle

This deep ditch is called a trench.

Melting crust

Sometimes, one plate plunges underneath another one. Part of it goes into the hot mantle, where it melts into magma.

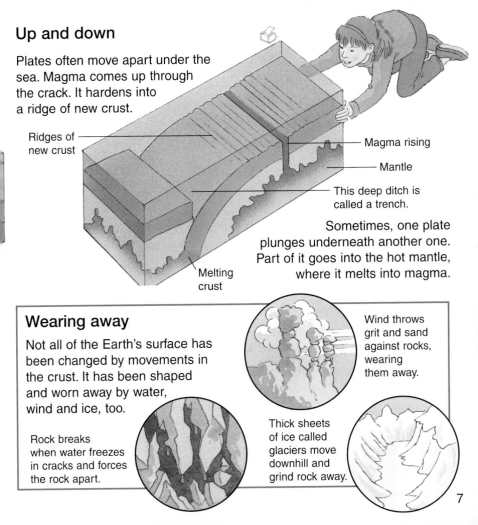

Wearing away

Not all of the Earth's surface has been changed by movements in the crust. It has been shaped and worn away by water, wind and ice, too.

Rock breaks when water freezes in cracks and forces the rock apart.

Wind throws grit and sand against rocks, wearing them away.

Thick sheets of ice called glaciers move downhill and grind rock away.

7

Earthquakes

An earthquake is when the Earth's crust shakes. Big earthquakes are violent and do lots of damage.

What happens?

Most earthquakes happen at plate boundaries. If the plates push against each other, the rocks get squeezed so hard that they sometimes slip or break. This makes vibrations, called shock waves, go through the rocks.

The place where the crust splits like this is called a fault.

The place underground where the first movement happens is called the focus of the earthquake.

On the surface, the place right above the focus is called the epicentre.*

These lines show shock waves moving out through the rocks.

*US = epicenter

Internet links Go to **www.usborne-quicklinks.com** for links to websites where you can find out more about earthquakes and set off your own quake.

Measuring earthquakes

The Mercalli scale is a list of 12 things which scientists look for that tell them how strong an earthquake is. As the numbers get higher, the damage gets worse.

At number 3 on the scale, hanging objects swing.

At number 8, towers and chimneys collapse.

At number 12, nearly everything is damaged. Big areas of land slip and move.

Animal warnings

Animals have been known to behave strangely before some earthquakes. In China, mice left their holes and ran in all directions.

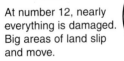

Making shock waves

Machines called seismometers can feel shock waves on the other side of the Earth. Try this experiment to make shock waves for yourself.

Place a piece of paper near the edge of a table and put a little salt in the middle.

Slip one end of a ruler under the paper. Hold the ruler gently, as shown in the picture.

Hit the other end of the ruler to make shock waves go along it. See the salt jump.

Volcanoes

Sometimes, red hot magma from the Earth's mantle pushes its way up into weak places in the crust. Then, it bursts through to the surface. As it cools, it hardens and forms a volcano. You can see what is going on inside this erupting volcano.

Clouds of steam, dust and ash rise high into the air.

This opening is called a crater.

Magma forces its way up this tube, called a vent.

Magma finds different ways out.

Magma was trapped in this underground chamber.

Magma which reaches the surface is called lava.

Lava cools and hardens into volcanic rock.

Layers of lava and ash build up each time the volcano erupts.

Ancient beliefs

In Roman times, people believed that volcanoes erupted because Vulcan, their god of fire, was making thunderbolts for the god Jupiter.

Different shapes

Many volcanoes are tall cones. This is because their lava is thick and sticky. It does not flow far before it hardens.

Cone volcano

Some volcanoes are fairly flat. Their lava is runny and flows before it cools.

Shield volcano

Volcanic rock

Pumice is a very light volcanic rock. It forms when lava hardens with gas bubbles trapped inside it.

You can buy pumice in health shops, for rubbing away hard skin.

Underwater volcanoes

There are lots of volcanoes under the sea because that is where the Earth's crust is the most thin and weak. Some islands are huge volcanoes which poke out of the water.

Dead or alive?

A live, or active, volcano erupts fairly often. A sleeping, or dormant, one rests for a long time between eruptions. A dead, or extinct, volcano is one which will never erupt again.

Edinburgh Castle in Scotland is built on the remains of an extinct volcano.

Internet links Go to **www.usborne-quicklinks.com** for links to websites where you can explore a volcano and take a volcano quiz.

11

Heat and power

The Earth's crust gives us
lots of the heat and power
we use in our homes,
schools, offices and
factories. Here are some
of the ways this happens.

Making hot water

In places with volcanoes, the rocks in
the crust are very hot. They can make
underground water boil and turn into steam.

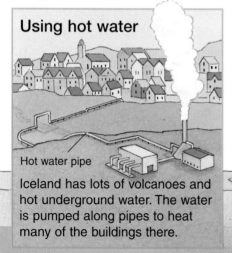

Using hot water

Hot water pipe

Iceland has lots of volcanoes and
hot underground water. The water
is pumped along pipes to heat
many of the buildings there.

A geyser is a jet
of hot water and
steam which shoots
out of the ground.

A hot spring is
where heated water
bubbles up through
cracks, to the surface.

Hot rock

Steam power

Some countries make electricity using steam from the Earth's crust.

Steam is trapped in this rock.

The steam goes along pipes to a building called a power station.

In the power station, the steam pushes the blades of a machine around, to make electricity.

Underground fuel

Coal, oil and gas are called fossil fuels. They form very slowly in the crust. Coal is the remains of plants that died millions of years ago.

Oil and gas are made from the remains of tiny sea animals and plants. Fossil fuels are used in some power stations to make electricity.

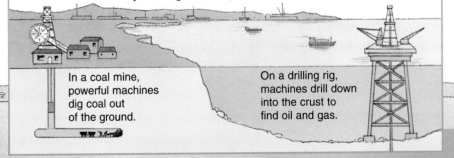

In a coal mine, powerful machines dig coal out of the ground.

On a drilling rig, machines drill down into the crust to find oil and gas.

Internet link Go to **www.usborne-quicklinks.com** for a link to a website where you can watch short animations about how crude oil was formed.

13

Igneous rock

The Earth's crust is made up of three main kinds of rocks. Igneous rock is one of them. It is made when magma rises from the mantle, then cools and hardens. "Igneous" means fiery.

Volcanoes are made from igneous rock. They make more rock each time they erupt.

Sometimes, magma cools and hardens into a huge mass of igneous rock under the ground.

Magma

Granite

Granite is a very hard igneous rock which forms under the ground.

In some places, big lumps of granite stick out of the ground. They were buried once, but the soil and rock above wore away.

Granite is good for building because it is hard and strong.

Sedimentary rock

The Earth's rocky crust is being worn away all the time. The tiny, worn fragments help to make new rock called sedimentary rock.

Fragments of rock can get washed into lakes, rivers and the sea. When they settle they are called sediment.

Layers of sediment

Squeezed bottom layers

Layers of sediment pile up slowly. The bottom layers get squeezed together to form sedimentary rock.

Layer upon layer

There are lots of layers of sedimentary rock in the Grand Canyon, in Arizona, America.

Sandstone

Sandstone is a sedimentary rock made from grains of sand from lakes, beaches or deserts.

You can often see layers in sandstone.

Sandstone is used for building, but it can be worn away by the weather.

New sandstone carving

Old sandstone carving

Internet link Go to **www.usborne-quicklinks.com** for a link to a website where you can follow the journey of a rock in a clickable rock cycle.

Metamorphic rock

Metamorphic rock starts life as igneous or sedimentary rock. It is made when these kinds of rocks are squeezed or heated, or both.

When mountains form, all the squeezing and heating makes huge amounts of metamorphic rock.

Magma can make the rock around it so hot that it changes into metamorphic rock.

This rock is not changing because it is not being heated.

Different kinds

Slate is a brittle metamorphic rock which splits easily. Thin sheets of it are used to make roof tiles.

Marble is a metamorphic rock which is often carved to make works of art. It comes in different shades.

Rock spotting

You can find different kinds of rocks almost anywhere. Here are some good places to start looking.

Mountains and hills usually have lots of bare rock and loose stones.

Many beaches are covered with pebbles. These are worn pieces of rock.

Buildings, statues and pavements are all made from different kinds of rocks.

Important notes

Never go alone.

Never go near dangerous places such as cliffs and deep water.

Always tell an adult where you are going.

Only collect loose rocks. Never break any off.

Things to take

These things will be useful when you go rock spotting.

A camera for recording things you see in towns.

A notebook and pencil for listing facts about each sample and where you found it.

Small plastic bags for collecting samples.

Felt-tip pens for numbering samples.

A book about rocks to help you find out what your samples are called.

Internet links Go to **www.usborne-quicklinks.com** for links to websites where you can watch a short movie about rocks and find out more about rock collecting.

17

Minerals

All rocks are made up of building blocks, called minerals. Minerals come in different shapes, sizes and shades. They form crystals which grow packed tightly together.

This is rock seen through a powerful microscope. The shapes are mineral crystals.

Different mixtures

Most rocks are made from a mixture of minerals. Granite is made from three minerals, but it can have different amounts of each one in it. This is why there are different kinds of granite. Here are three of them.

Big crystals

If minerals have plenty of space to grow, they can become beautiful flat-sided crystals.

Amethyst

Pyrite

You can sometimes find rocks with crystals growing inside, like this.

Minerals around us

Minerals are taken out of the ground and used to make all kinds of things that we use every day. Can you find any of these things in your home?

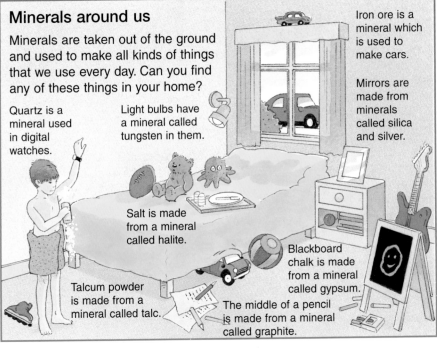

Iron ore is a mineral which is used to make cars.

Mirrors are made from minerals called silica and silver.

Quartz is a mineral used in digital watches.

Light bulbs have a mineral called tungsten in them.

Salt is made from a mineral called halite.

Blackboard chalk is made from a mineral called gypsum.

Talcum powder is made from a mineral called talc.

The middle of a pencil is made from a mineral called graphite.

Gemstones

Gemstones are mineral crystals which have been cut into special shapes and polished. They are very hard. They are also beautiful and expensive.

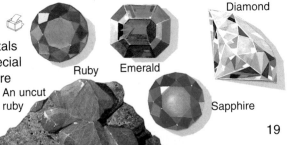

Ruby

Emerald

Diamond

An uncut ruby

Sapphire

19

Caves

In some places, there are huge caves and tunnels under the ground. They have been carved out by water, which has soaked into the soil and rock, from the Earth's surface.

Rainwater and water from streams and rivers soak into the ground.

Soaking in

Rock which has tiny spaces or cracks in it lets water trickle through. Any rock which lets water through is called permeable rock.

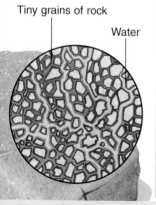

Tiny grains of rock

Water

Sponge test

A bath sponge has spaces in it, rather like permeable rock. Try this experiment to see how water soaks through the spaces. It works best if you wet the sponge then squeeze it out first.

Put the sponge on a plate and pour water on slowly. Stop when the water starts trickling out.

To see how much water has soaked into the sponge's spaces, squeeze it over an empty jug.

Internet link Go to **www.usborne-quicklinks.com** for a link to a website where you can take a virtual tour of some underground caves and find out how they were formed.

Carving out

Limestone rock is made up of layers. Cracks between the layers let water trickle through.

As the water trickles, it eats away at the rock. Very slowly the cracks become tunnels.

When water wears away big areas of rock, a cave is made.

Stalactites and stalagmites

Water drips from a cave roof and leaves behind tiny amounts of minerals. Very slowly, these form rocky icicles called stalactites. Drops hit the floor and towers called stalagmites form.

Stalactites hang down from the cave roof.

A potholer explores caves.

Stalactites and stalagmites can join up to make a pillar.

Stalagmites grow up from the cave floor.

21

Fossils

Scientists have found out what lived on Earth millions of years ago by studying fossils. Fossils are mostly found in sedimentary rock.

How fossils form

When an animal dies, its soft parts rot away but its hard skeleton is left. If it sinks into a muddy place, it gets covered with sediment.

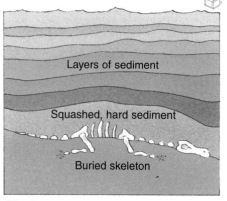

Layers of sediment

Squashed, hard sediment

Buried skeleton

The bottom layers become squashed and harden into rock. Over time, minerals in the rock turn the skeleton to stone. This makes it into a fossil.

Finding fossils

People who study fossils are called palaeontologists. Take a close look next time you go to a rocky beach and you may find some fossils yourself.

Fossils are usually found when the rock around them gets worn away.

Pick up stones and turn them over to take a good look.

If you want to look at a really good fossil collection, contact your nearest museum to see what they have.

Internet links

For links to more websites about the Earth, go to the Usborne Quicklinks Website at **www.usborne-quicklinks.com** and click on the number of the website you want to visit.

Website 1 – Explore an online exhibit that looks at rocks above and below the surface of the Earth and find out more about mining. You can also discover different types of rocks and minerals that are used to make roads and cars.

Website 2 – A fun introduction to the Earth where you can meet young and old rocks, learn what a volcano scientist does and find ideas for things to make and do at home.

Website 3 – See a different picture of the Earth every day or browse an archive of incredible photographs.

Website 4 – Discover where volcano eruptions are taking place around the world and find lots of volcano facts and photographs.

Website 5 – Not all fossils are dinosaur skeletons and on this interesting site, you can find out what a fossil is, explore a clickable timeline and see lots of pictures of different kinds of fossils - even fossil poo!

Website 6 – This entertaining and informative site about rocks and minerals is packed with advice for junior rockhounds and features online activities and fun illustrations.

Index

First published in 2002 by Usborne Publishing Ltd., Usborne House, 83-85 Saffron Hill, London EC1N 8RT, England. www.usborne.com Copyright © 2002, 1995 Usborne Publishing Ltd. The name Usborne and the device ♀ ⊕ are Trade Marks of Usborne Publishing Ltd. All rights reserved. No part of this publication may be reproduced, stored in a retrieval system, or transmitted in any form or by any means, electronic, mechanical, photocopying, recording, or otherwise, without the prior permission of the publisher. UE First published in America 2002. Printed in China.